CW00342340

Diverse Ditties

Diverse Ditties

William R. Torvaney

The Pentland Press Limited
Edinburgh • Cambridge • Durham • USA

First published in 1997 by
The Pentland Press Ltd.
1 Hutton Close
South Church
Bishop Auckland
Durham

British Library Cataloguing in Publication Data.
A catalogue record for this book is available
from the British Library.

ISBN 1 85821 529 3

Typeset by CBS, Felixstowe, Suffolk
Printed and bound by Bookcraft Ltd, Bath

THREE HORS D'OEUVRES

'Choose we for life's weapon
Harp or sword or pen,
Perish every sluggard,
Let us all be men.'

Alfred Earl.

'But howsoever rich the store,
I'd lay it down
To feel upon my back once more
The old red gown.'

R.F. Murray.

'Then back come the pier and the
cliffs and the castle
And back comes the morn with its
burden rue
Bej, does the mist still hang round
the College
Bej, is the blue of the Bay still
as blue?'

J.B. Salmond.

CONTENTS

* *Military cloth: eventually became Khaki!*

Other Verses written in War-time

Other verses – since leaving France

INTRODUCTION

I suppose that I have been aware of these works from my early teens, when studying English at school and looking for something to read at home that was 'different'.

I developed an affinity for several of them over the years, as I hope you will too. Having been used to reading them in faded typewritten format on yellowing paper, to re-read them again in crisp and clear typeface on white paper was like discovering a whole new set of poems. I found the effect quite moving as I could picture the author stoking his favourite pipe with a tobacco blend, Chaplain's Choice, named by him for a local blender in Aberdeen, then settling down to read his own work, in its new format, with a studious smile on his face.

Ian L. Torvaney

MY GIRL

I

My love is young and wondrous fair
Fair as a morn in May,
The tendrils of her auburn hair
Round her sweet forehead play,
A light shines in her sweet blue eyes
I trust it shines for me
Flawless as any Cornish skies
Deeper than any sea.

II

My love is gracious, true and kind,
And when she smiles on me
The vibrant fibres of my mind
Tremble in ecstasy,
She is a pearl beyond all price,
The darling of my heart
And may the cast of Fortune's dice
Grant that we never part.

College Echoes 20.11.14

TO A SPRITE

I

Comfort my aching heart
Thou sprite of the haunted bogland
Guide me through all the paths
Of Leaming's weary fogland
Aye! when the day is done
And the dying sun
Floods all the earth with blood-red streams
Come to me in my dreams.

II

Give me a moment's space
In the dank wet mist o'er the sedges
Give me that searching look
That all my badness dredges.
Aye! when chill night lets fall
Its velvet pall
Purge me and make me clear of all that tends
To lose the best of friends.

College Echoes 5.12.15.

EYES OF GREY

Two eyes of bluey-grey
Wayward and fair to look upon
As reek o' the peat,
Wicked or wistful
Jaded or joyous
But ever sweet.

Two eyes of bluey-grey,
Tranquil and crystal clear
As pools of the summer sea,
Gaze o'er the shingly beach,
And joy that can ne'er be numbed
Comes over me.

Two eyes of bluey-grey
Dreamless and full of meaning
As smoke of the battle-plain;
Eyes that will never be
Dim in my memory
Steadfast they reign.

College Echoes 29.1.15.

SONG OF THE GLEEMAN

(Beowulf 89-100)

There was the music of the harp
The song of the gleeman grey,
Telling the story of earth's own birth
And the dawn of man's first day;
Telling of mountains and boundless plains
And the great sea girdling round,
And the sun and moon in the firmament
'Mid radiant glory crowned,
Singing of trees with the leafy boughs
And the creatures great and small.

So the king's men joyed exceedingly
That night in Heriot's Hall.

A REQUIEM

When Time shall turn to me and say
'You Sir have had your little day,
But one last sip of wine – like Life
Then leave this world of stress and strife.'
Friends, when the last dread hour has come,
And these my lips are cold and dumb,
Let no production of masonic art,
A broken obelisk, a chiselled heart,
Mar the fair landscape where I lie,
A grassy mound suffices me, hard by
A bunch of pale forget-me-nots, which like the skies,
Rival but ne'er outshine her sweet blue eyes.

College Echoes 26.2.15.

GREEN?

I

She said her eyes were green,
A ruthless calumny.
He swore that they were blue,
Of lovely lucent hue;
Exchanged fibs not a few;
She said her eyes were green
As any onion bree.

II

The moon somehow got lost
Behind a filmy cloud
He struck a match that he might see
Twin sapphires blue as the summer sea
She blew it out with girlish glee;
The moon no longer being lost
Right slily smiled aloud.

College Echoes 16.3.15.

THE NIGHT BREEZE

I

Down by the water-side
Where the stately cygnets glide
Since this old world began
Resort of maid and man
At eventide.
There's where I long to be
Just once again to see
The sunset's rosy glow
The happy wavelets flow
Careless and free.

II

Breeze of the beauteous wild
But rightly art thou styled
A breath of Nature's balm,
For in thy sacred calm
Is wiled
Away all grief and pain
Ne'er to return again.
Exult ye cherubim above
For joy and peace and love
Have come to reign.

College Echoes 12.2.15.

DUSK

I

Up on the wind-swept heights
Far from the bookworm's lair
When the soft dusk falls like a velvet shroud,
And e'en our voices ring too loud
In the frosty air.

II

Silent we stand and gaze
At the twinkling lights through the haze
As the starlight glimmers on the bay
Awed at our thoughts we wend our way
Down the steep brae.

College Echoes 5.2.15.

A TRIBUTE

(Respectfully dedicated to Sir James Donaldson)

Scholar and courtly gentleman
Honoured by one and all
Thought and deed that is best in us
Answer thy spirit's call,
As we turn to see thee standing
Lit by the sunset ray
In the quiet gray gloaming
Of your life's long day.

College Echoes 5.12.15.

MOODS

I

When the brain is tired
And the written word looks cold
When the thought inspired
Is far as unmined gold
I want to climb a mountain's
  sun-kissed crest
      And rest.

II

When the heart is fired
And pen has super-might
When things desired
Would seem to shape aright
Then could I shout a glorious
  refrain
      And start again.

III

When the cheek is flushed
With draughts of wine
When all care is crushed
And every joy seems mine
Then in my dreams I roam in
  fancy free
      With thee.

ACROSS THE NIGHT

I

Across the night you cry to me
My lady of the faithless eyes,
Across the night I fly to thee
Tho' Hope within most nearly dies
And in my dreams I seem to hear your voice
        Laughing, jesting
        Never resting
But far beyond my reach as are the skies.

II

All thro' the night you speak to me
My lady of the ripe, red lips,
All thro' the night I yearn to open,
Those crimson doors whose locks none slips
And as I lie awake I hear your laugh
        Tinkling, never ceasing
        My desire increasing
But far away from me as phantom ships.

UNLESS

I

Unless you come with me
Across the meadows of Life's happy morn
Unless you're by my side
My daily toil is weary and forlorn
Unless your sunny smile
Shines radiant from those tender eyes of grey
I live in loneliness
With Home far, far away.

II

Unless I win your heart
And kindle love-fires in your gracious eyes
'Twere best that we should part
And I find solace 'neath the southern skies.
But if you come to me
With tender glance and shy caress
Then in pure ecstasy
I'll prove my love for thee, unless!

Cannock Chase.

WHEN FIRST WE MET

I

When first I saw the sunshine in your hair
My heart beat high and all the world seemed bright,
When first I knew the radiance of your smile
My soul brimmed o'er with Love's first sweet delight,
No star in all the sky shone half so fair
As you upon that scented summer morn
The sun soft-shining on your goldenhair
When first we met amid the golden corn.

II

When first I heard the music of your voice
And saw your sweet lips part in speech to me
'Twas then I knew that I might well rejoice
In bonds of Love that would for ever be,
'Twas then I saw the whiteness of your soul
As of some angel from the realms divine
'Twas then I held the heaven of your heart
And knew at last that heart was ever mine.

Cannock Chase.

MY LASSIE

My lassie's eyes are like the skies
Of joyous nights in June,
When stars above look down in love
And rival with the moon;
My lassie's smile I value more
Than wealth of previous gems galore;
Her shy caress, her answering kiss,
They yield an argosy of bliss.

My lassie's lips are like the doors
Of some fair shrine that's rubied o'er;
That must be touched with reverence
To view aright the golden store.
My lassie's heart is sweet and whole,
And dear to me as my own soul:
And all my life I'll keep her love,
While there's a God in Heaven above.

MA DAME D.P.

I

I wandered out alone one autumn eve
Through fragrant meads, besprinkled all with dew,
While fleecy clouds cursed the soft-dying day
'Mid universal tinge of purple hue;
I sat me down to rest upon a stile
That I might view this peaceful scene awhile.

II

I dreamed a dream, a maiden beauteous fair
With eyes of violet-blue and golden hair,
Stole my poor heart, nay reader, do not smile
For though I followed many a weary mile
In her fair footsteps, yet she proved untrue,
To me who sought her, many another too.

III

You faithless jade! thy memory still I keep
And oft when wrapt in toils of peaceful sleep
I dream of thee, and sometimes call to mind
Thy hair soft-lifted by the winnowing wind,
Like wisps of gold, oft I have pined
To clasp thy soft hand and soothe thy troubled cries
And gaze deep into thy peerless eyes.

IV

'Frailty thy name is Woman' saith the Bard
Man, too, is sometimes frail, exams are hard
When one is unprepared; oh may I be
Hereafter worthier of 'Ma Dame D.P.'

College Echoes Nov. 21st 1913.

(D.P. is Varsity slang for the ordinary Class Certificate of having 'duly performed' the work of the class.)

CROSSING THE BAR

RUGGER

When the other side is waiting
And the leather's at your toe
And you hoof it like a beggar
Just with every ounce you know
What a joy it is to goal it
'Tween the posts to see it go
Crossing the bar.

HOCKEY

When you're playing centre-forward
And the goalie's there to beat,
And you feel a bally hero
With the pilule at your feet,
Then you lift it right above the bar,
And colour up like beet,
Crossing the bar.

BILLIARDS

When you're playing in the Final
For fifteen bob or so
And the other – beastly rotter
Calmly sinks your globule low
Then leaves the pills in 'double-baulk'

How wild you see it go
Crossing the bar.

'A' CERTIF.

I

When you see a wretched semi
Trying hard to drill a squad
While a swagger spatted captain
Stands grousing in the Quad
You can bet your bottom dollar
As you hear that semi holler
That his limbs are beastly stiff
And he's sitting 'A' Certif.

II

What visions of that fifteen bob
Which he will get at camp
To spend on pleasant remedies
For keeping out the damp.
Oh it's rotten to be drilling
The suspense is simply thrilling
When your brain box turns to tripe
For a bloomin' lance's stripe.

III

It's the aim of many a josser,
When he joins the O.T.C.,

To become a bally sergeant
By getting through his ‘B’
Tho’ he thinks he’s jolly cute,
There’s a chance he’ll get the boot,
For he’ll find it jolly stiff
When he’s sitting ‘A’ Certif.

College Echoes 14.11.13.

CONFESSIO IN POCULIS

I

Oh! some men call for Burgundy
For chartreuse or champagne
The luscious wines of Normandy
Dark port from sunny Spain.
My tastes are more plebeian
It may seem rather queer
Before the finest vintage
I'd drink my lager beer.

II

Oh! some men smoke Abdullahs
De Reszke and State Express
Gourdonlis and Ariston
Expensive brands – no less.
But my purse is too slender
Excepting now and then,
To smoke but cheap Virginians
At coppers three for ten.

III

Oh! some men rave of maidens
Tall and divinely fair
With limpid eyes and ruby lips
And glistening golden hair

But my ideal maiden
Will laugh and dance and sing
And make at least one fellow
As happy as a king.

College Echoes 12.12.13.

AD INCOGNITAM

I

Oh! maiden of the auburn hair
And dimpled cheek beyond compare
And eyes of azure hue
I ne'er adored a maiden fair
Till Fortune showed me you.

II

You trip the light fantastic toe
With nymph-like lissomness, and so
My pulse beats like a dynamo
When valsing it with you.
When errant tendrils of your hair
Tickled my neck, I do declare
'Twas more than mortal man might dare
To seek those eyes of blue.

III

I wrote a sonnet ere I slept
To dream of you. But Eros crept
Athwart the brinklady who kept
The fire alight with my
Somewhat faint praises of your grace
Your queenly head and lovely face,
'Tis not the time nor yet the place
To drivel more – Good-bye.

Christmas Number – *College Echoes* 1913

BETTY

I

I know a lass – a bonny lass
With ruby lips and raven locks
And her I love right truly,
And when we part my stricken heart
With undue haste invades my socks
My temper gets unruly.

II

Her name is Bet, her Pa's a vet
Who drives a motor landaulette
From morn till dewy eve.
He doctors dogs – she fractures hearts
With Epsom salts – and Cupid's darts,
At least I so believe.

III

I like that girl, on her I'm bent,
She's got the 'dibs' she'd pay the rent
And run the whole kerboosh
But don't you see she won't agree
To think of me sans £.s.d.,
And so I've got the push.

Christmas Number – *College Echoes* 1913

A DREAM

I

The stag at eve had drunk his fill
And so had Snooks. No silver rill
In undiluted state had slaked his thirst
And as he slept he dreamed that he
Was flying on a swift B.E.,
And straining hard to reach St. Andrews first.
    Then the engine thudded
    And the biplane scudded
        Blinding along
        Grinding along
Through the mist and the wind and the night.

II

At 8 p.m. he'd left the 'Plain'
And started out through wind and rain
Cursing his luck like the mate of a tramp
Vowing he'd beat the night express
Before the folk had time to dress
Or boldly ventured out into the damp.
    So the engine thudded
    And the biplane scudded
        Haring' along
        Tearing along
Like a ghost through the wind and the night.

III

The wee grey city hove in sight
A wraith-like town in the morning light
And only sleepy 'coppers' paced the street.
With a smash and a crash the biplane
Into the college Tower was smashed
The whole concern at Coutt's naked feet.
    So the engine stopped
    And the pilot dropped
        Falling down
        Bawling down
Through the mist and the wind and the night.

Envoi

And when he awoke
He scarcely could croak
He'd fallen out of bed
Had a mighty sore head
As he lay on the floor
With gusts he swore.

College Echoes 30.1.14..

AN O.T.C. SONG

Suggested tune 'Johnny comes marching home'.

I

When first you come a bejant to this little Varsitee
You've got a sort of notion that you're after a Degree
But then the Sergeant comes in sight
With his baggy breeches and buttons bright
    And before you can scoot
    You've become a recruit
    In the Varsity O.T.C.

Refrain:

    Yes before you can scoot
    You've become a recruit
    In the Varsity O.T.C.

II

Of course you hate the dull parades that come at first
Route marches teach you what it is to have a thirst
But when at last you get to camp
And the bally old tent lets in the damp
    You troll out a song
    To show you belong
    To the Varsity O.T.C.

Refrain:

Yes you troll out a song
To show you belong
To the Varsity O.T.C.

III

Now, when the Kaiser tries to make old Britain
bite the dust
We've got to do our little bit
In fact we know we must
So we wire at once to 'Captain Rob'
Saying we're on for an Army job
And we're jolly well glad
For the time we've had
In the Varsity O.T.C.

Refrain:

Yes, we're jolly glad
For the time we've had
In the Varsity O.T.C.

College Echoes 30.10.14.

DRAW IT MILD

I stood upon that broad expanse of gold
Kissed by cerulean waters of the bay,
And with my stick upon the sand full bold
I traced her name, and after it the day.
With proud exultant step I turned to go
Back to the wee grey town and café tea;
The cruel careless waves rolled up and lo!
Her name was blotted out. Then rose in me
A tumult of vain wrath. Oh! fickle sand
And feeble stick and treacherous tide who pose
As mankind's henchmen with this my right hand
I'll ------

I'll steer the biggest aeroplane
Across the beastly bounding main,
And take the tallest tree that grows
Stick it in Etna for a dose
Of sulphur. Then that night, write
'Mid stench of smoke and flame I'll
Across the vast blue firmament
Her name – 'twill surely make a dent
That safe beyond all human doubt
No D----d wave can ever wash it out.

College Echoes 30.10.14.

CHUCKED! – A Tragic Episode

There was a youth
Of tastes quixotic
Who verses wrote
On themes erotic.
He occupied a dingy attic
His metres were a bit erratic
Some stuff he wrote
To you I'll quote:
'Nymph of the north
Queen of my heart
Fresh as the North Sea foam
Through the wild woods
Through the sweet meads
Joyous with thee I'll roam.'

She was indignant, said 'Beware,
It isn't fair to praise my hair
And criticise my lips and eyes
In public print. Pray take the hint
And from this day don't look my way.'

The poet swore
He'd write no more
And in despair
He climbed the stair
And tore his hair.

And if you care
You'll find him there.

College Echoes 30.10.14

GAZETTED

I

Not so very long ago
Just how long I scarcely know
When 'Bloody Bill' the Kaiser kicked the traces,
I decided that I'd fight
All the day and all the night
And try to smash some ugly German faces.

II

So I wrote my old C.O.
Saying that I'd like to go
Wherever junior Subalterns were wanted.
Sent my application in
Passed the Doctor with a grin
For I guessed my heart and lungs were strongly planted.

III

After many weary weeks
When one scarcely ever speaks
Except to curse the lucks who keep us waiting
I'm just off my nut with glee
For we're off to Camberley
Where we'll have to undergo full many a slating.

IV

Well, perhaps we'll all come back,
When we've had our little wack,
At the foe whose power old Britain's bent on breaking,
So let those we've left behind
Keep their poor old pals in mind
Tho' we're dead against the fuss that folk are making.

College Echoes 27.11.14.

GAMALIELLE

I

We know a maiden chic très belle
Her name it is Gamalielle
She lectures us with intent fell
    On tongues antique
For Anglo-Saxon is her job
We somehow guess it's not her hob
Our muddled intellects to rob
    Just twice a week.

II

And why? No aptitude have we
For stan and ic as far's I see
We'll never even smell Degree
    Unless maybe
We bask beneath her gracious smile
And yielding to her winsome wile
We learn our stuff in better style
    Tho' not with glee.

III

Tho' at her feet we cannot swot
As pious Greeks would do, I wot

Yet still we learn a fairish lot
    And fairish well
So when we're floundering through 'Cook'
And at vocabs, we furtive look
Smile at us sweetly o'er your book
    Gamalielle.

College Echoes 27.11.14.

REJECTED

I

Oft in the night
When all is hushed and still
Oft in the night
Woo sommes how I will
The brutal short refrain
Throbs ever in my brain
        Rejected!

II

Oft in the night
I think of men who've gone
Through memory's mist
I see them every one
        with far better luck than I
        whom we gave a boisterous good-bye
            Our hearts dejected.

III

Oft in the night
I curse the cruel Fates
And with grey dawn
My anger scarce abates

To think that we who long to go are stayed
All eager that our country's debt be paid
And yet; God and the King obeyed
        Rejected!

College Echoes 14.12.14.

MEMORIES

I

Memories nursed by the firelight glow
Balm to the weary brain
Welcome to flagging wits of man
As wine to the sunny plain.
Pictures fair of days that are done,
Flit across Memory's screen,
Stabbing the heart with a vain regret
For the things that 'might have been'.
Stirring the embers of youth's desire
A glimpse of the heart's own Queen.

Refrain:
When the mist is on the mountains
and the day is on the wane
When the winter wind is sobbing
It's weirdly sweet refrain.

II

Hearsed in the clammy mist of years
Wraith-like faces come,
Furrowed with grief that outlives tears
Grief that is tense and numb.
The fancy flits to a brighter sphere
When Love's own sunlight shines,

Bathing the heart with a rosy glow
Sweetest of anodynes,
And under the spell of her clear grey eyes
An ardent soul reclines.

Refrain:
When the mist's on Benachallie
And the snow is under foot
When the winter morn's reveille
Is the quaver of the coot.

III

Thoughts of a callow bijanthood
Days when we worked and played
With a zest and buoyant thoughtlessness
Rambles through hough and glade,
Ere Bellona's dread call sounded
Through Scotland's farthest glen,
And the King's highway resounded
With the tramp of marching men,
Ere the bloody plains of Belgium
Lay stark with our ken.

Refrain:
When the mist hangs round the College
And the winter night is chill
Yet hot Hell's afoot in Flanders
Lusting slaughter and to kill.

College Echoes 29.1.15.

SPRAY

I

Glint of the spring-fraught sunlight,
Wave of the wild North Sea,
Spray that flashes round the Spindle
Dear to the heart of me.
Crag and breaker and pierhead,
Mist o'er the morning bay
Wrenching the cloak of sable
Just for the nonce away.

II

Would that through Life's short journey
Each day and night be spent
With the winds and the waves and the woodlands
And the great sky for our tent,
For whether we bask in the sunlight
Or gasp in the rude March gale
There's a glorious zest that stirs us
When Pleasure's minions fail.

College Echoes 16.3.15.

THOUGHTS

(Based on Anne of Austria's speech in '*The Three Musketeers*' beginning 'Man forgets, woman remembers-')

Forget – you say – forget?
How can I cast aside
Into oblivion's tide
Deeds that have stained my scutcheon fair,
Slights that are brutal hard to bear?
You ask it, and I'll answer,
Yes! I can
For I'm a man.

Remember – did you say – remember?
Aye! more's the pity on't,
Woman remembers only what is worst
After the vehemence of wrath's storm has burst
The bonds of love asunder,
And hate's dreadful thunder
Through weary months and years
'Remember!'

Woman repents
Then man but regrets
At thought of unpaid debt,
Though Fate's obdurate sway
Ordain a long delay,
Man can – and will – repay.

College Echoes 19.2.15.

10th MARCH 1915

(Official Memorial Poem on the death of Principal Sir James Donaldson.)

The Angel of Death with wings outspread
Flew o'er the city grey
And stole from our midst our well loved Chief
In the dusk of his life's long day.

Scholar and courtly gentleman
Loved by us one and all
Thought and deed that is best in us
Answer thy spirit's call.

Thou art gone on thy last long journey
To the Halls of the Ever Blest
But thy memory lives in the loyal hearts
Of those whom you loved the best.

Rest, noble heart, for ever
Long hast thou lived – and well –
Till the charm of Death is bridged across
At the sound of the last dread knell.

JULY 1916

Last night we heard the mighty guns roar forth
Deep throated challenge: from the hard-held North
Above the wet stark plains of Flanders, down
To shambled Verdun, each ill-fated town
Of bruited name through death of friend or foe
Trembled amid her ruins, where two years ago
When all was peaceful, God had seemed so kind,
And no black thought of War had seared the mind
At nightfall still o'er France's stricken plain
Come din and clangour of fair cities slain.

This poem was written in bed at the 25 Casualty Cl. Statn. Aubigny, on the night of June 30th 1916 when the great British bombardment was at its height.

THE COBBLED ROAD

I

Now this is a tale the poplars tell
Of the road to Armentières,
Where we marched right up to the gates of Hell,
Off and on for a couple of years.

II

One weary march o'er the cobbled stones,
When we couldn't breathe for heat;
When we cursed our luck with blistering tongues,
And we cursed our blistered feet,
We passed by a little latticed house
With a creeper on the wall,
And a Flemish girl who waved her hand;
My God! how it cheered us all.

III.

A long march o'er the cobbled stones,
Through the silent poplar trees,
In the clammy mist of an autumn dawn,
And a whiff of a rancid breeze;
But the latticed house is shattered now,
And the creepers bruised and torn,
And no maid smiled us a bright good-day,
As we past in the still grey morn.

IV

There's many a tale the poplars tell
Of that road of cobbled stone,
Where Bill and I marched side by side,
And I came back alone.

(In the vernacular of the British soldier Armentières is pronounced 'Armenteers'.)

(*Daily Chronicle* Oct. 20th 1916.)

THE GALLANT FORTY-TWA

I

You've heard the folk praise the Seaforths
Or laud the Gordons gay
The sturdy Scottish Rifles
Frae mony a Lowland brae,
But if ye see men marching
Wi' sober steady tread
The swing of kilts
Of sombre hue
Wi' hackle red
An' bonnet blue
In a' the land there's nane sae braw
As oor Black Watch, the Forty-Twa.

II

There's mony a lad frae Scotia's glens
That wears the bonnet blue,
An' mony a lad of valiant heart
Has braved a morn of rue
For glory of a nameless clan
Mid skirl of pipes while foemen ran
Frae swirl of kilts
Of sombre hue
Frae hackle red
An' bonnet blue

While brave men stand and brave men fa'
They're oor Black Watch, the Forty-Twa.

PARCELS

I

We've just come from the trenches!
Now listen to my tale;
Though we're weary,
Eyes all bleary.
Weather dreary,
Still we're cheery,
For we've come down from the trenches,
And we've got our parcels mail.

II

After bully-beef and biscuits,
After chlorinated tea,
Short of fags,
Clothes in rags,
Sleep by snatches,
Knees all scratches,
Every Jock is laughing, joking,
As the brazier he's stoking,
For we've come down from the trenches,
And we've got our parcels mail.

HAME

There's a wee bit cottage
Whaur I'd like fine tae be,
An' the wind blaws snell
Frae the grey North Sea;
Jist a lane wee hoosie
In a dreich braeside,
I can see my mither sittin'
By oor ain fireside.

There's a wee bit ribbon
On my auld green kilt,
There are twa frail hands
On a weel worn quilt;
There's a black tasselled sporran
On the ben room wa'
'Gin my laddie comes back
He maun look real braw.'

There's a hamesick laddie
On the plains o' France
An' he aye gies 'The Plough'
Sic a wistful glance;
For the war's sair trauchle
When the wind blaws cauld,
An' the lads coorie doon
Like the yowes in their fauld.

But the war's no finished,
We must e'en bide a wee,
Ye maun aye rob the kailyaird
Tae mak' halesome bree;
Till the hale thing's dune wi'
We'll a' hae tae bide
For our wee bit cottage
On a Scots braeside.

People's Friend
(Scottish Edition.)

'BLIGHTY'

There's a land more blessed than a shrine thrice blest,
There's a land more precious than the wealth o' the West,
Where each toil-stained warrior finds well-earned rest,
Whose Mother-call is mighty.
It's a land where each wanderer longs oft to be,
For there's welcome always and hearts care-free,
Where the surge flakes white from the grey North Sea,
On the shore that our lads call
'Blighty'.

It's a land o' fair cities and moorlands drear,
Where the cause of Freedom is aye held dear,
And her bruited name through climes far and near,
Stands firm by the King Almighty.
Though the night be long and the trail be lone,
And the North wind chills to the inmost bone
We can yet thank God for what's still our own;
That peerless island
'Blighty'.

In November fog or September sun
By Highland lochside where moorhens run
'Mid a city's roar when her toil's half-done
When War and Death seem mighty
When the West flames red at a long day's end
And night shrouds nations, false foe or fast friend

May our prayer still be that though worlds contend
We ne'er lose our homeland
'Blighty'.

Ripon Feb. 1917
Dundee Advertiser 16th Feb.

TO MY PIPE

I

Oh, trusted comrade of a thousand nights,
Oh, great producer of life's best delights,
The thought of days without thee sore affrights
This mundane mind of mine.
For pale-blue ringlets from thine ancient bowl
Have eased the troubled brain and soothed the soul
In darksome days you glowed like fires of coal,
With influence benign.

II

Men rave of paper-covered flimsy weed,
A cherished precious thing in days of need,
But when mankind requires a friend indeed
When time is ripe,
For deeds of derring-do by flood or field,
When eager armies shout and foemen yield,
When, blade and bomb we can no longer wield,
Give me my pipe.

Dundee Advertiser Sept. 12th 1917.

GLAUR

Sludge, sludge, sludge
Through the cold grey Artois mud;
Trudge, trudge, trudge,
'Mid the wail of a big Boche dud –
Folk call it 'GLAUR'.

Tramp, tramp, tramp
While the greasy 'duck-boards' creak;
Cramp, cramp, cramp,
Sleep snatched 'mid the trench rats' squeak;
Folk talk of 'GLAUR',
But this is 'WAUR'.

Crash, crash, crash,
As the shells go hurtling o'er us,
Smash, smash, smash,
At the grisly foe before us;
Folk talked of 'GLAUR',
But this is 'WAUR',
It's WAR!

Dundee Advertiser

Written in a canvas hut at Forceville before we went into the trenches opposite Beaumont Hamel.

UP THE LINE

This piece of verse was written originally in a cellar under a ruined village called Auchouvillers, two kilometres from Beaumont Hamel, which three weeks later was captured by the Highland Division.

I

There's a smoking, steamin' cooker,
An' some panting dixie-carriers,
An' the Sergeant-Major too;
For the winter dawn is breaking
An' the lads are late in waking
'Cos the piper's hands were blue.

II

There's a hurry and a hustling;
Can't you see the sergeant's bustling
Till the huts are fair and fine?
For the Highland lads are going.
Be it raining, be it snowing,
They're going up the line.

III

To the brimstone brink of Hades,
Where the path of duty laid is,
To the far, far distant Rhine,
Be it bayonets, bombing, shelling,
Or the gas-cloud evil smelling
They're going up the line.

TO A BRAZIER

Oh, battered, blackened biscuit tin,
Thy rude exterior seems
A solace to our snow-soaked limbs,
Progenitor of steams
I'd hug thine honest, ugly form
Were you not quite so hot;
Your grateful warmth has fired my veins
(Hence this poetic rot.)

Time was when you had silver sheen
And bulged with biscuits hard;
A Colonel's pail you might have been,
But now with visage marred,
By sundry rude entrenching tools
You crackle, fume, and glow,
To glad the hearts and fill the voids
Of Tommy, Jock, and Co.

You boil my mess-tin full of tea,
You thaw my frozen toes,
To realms more torrid than this earth
You relegate our woes,
So when the lads are clustered round,
E'en though the air seems hazier,
We'll drink your health in smoky tea,
Our grimy pal – the Brazier.

Dundee Advertiser, April 30th.

Ripon 1917.

STRAY THOUGHTS

Dusk and the sullen autumn sky
Looms o'er the trench scarred plain,
Grey Boreas with chilly sigh
Brings memories to the brain;
Wind of our Scottish northland dear,
Breath of our native moorland drear.

O'er marshy plains of Flanders
Come wafted thoughts of home;
Each mind from battle wanders
To breast the North Sea foam;
Each ice-cold breath inhaled revives the past
Ere at Bellona's feet the die was cast.

And then we turn to War's imperious toil,
To shattered trench or mangled wire;
And as we strive a cunning foe to foil,
We think from time to time of some home fire.
Blow, Boreas, and freeze War into Peace,
That wanton Death and Pestilence may cease.

Dundee Advertiser. November 21, 1916.

This poem was written in a dilapidated billet behind Hebuterne where we trained for a big push which did not come off.

SOCKS

I

Oh, great and glorious thought
That warms the heart of me;
Whence buoyant hope is brought
To pedal part of me,
        That pair of socks.

II

My weary feet are set
With warlike drudgery.
What helps me to forget
This endless 'trudgery'?
        That pair of socks.

III

My mother – kindly soul,
Has sent them out to me,
And from my open pack
They seem to say, you see,
        That pair of socks.

IV

What joy! I'm dry and clean again!
My feet feel wondrous warm,
I'm ready to go out again
In 'strafe' or gas alarm.
The psychologic fact is plain to me
That courage comes when feet from
    cold are free
        Thrice-blessed pair of socks.

30.12.16.

OUR TOFF

(Baron Hubert Julius de Reuter, a Private in 15 Platoon, 7th Black Watch was killed at Beaumont Hamel Nov. 13th 1916.)

We ’ad a toff in our platoon
A baron’s son was he,
A toff wot did his share of work
An’ drank his Army tea
An’ spent near all his handy cash
On chaps like you and me.

He might have been a red-tab swell
That’s wot he might have been,
But then we chaps that’s coarser-like
Would never quite ha’ seen
The splendid man he was right through
A soldier – straight and keen.

He’s gone – like many another chap
An’ we wot’s out here still
When grey dawn breaks and men ‘stand to’
When armies fight and kill
We misses ’Arry, our star toff,
Who lies near Mailly hill.

I ain’t religious, but I’d like
To thank the God who gave
This world our Harry, Baron’s son
Who found a soldier’s grave.

BEAUMONT HAMEL

Beaumont Hamel, Beaumont Hamel
Oh that thrice-accursed village
Where we gazed
All amazed
Saw you razed
God be praised!
There was little left for pillage
Beaumont Hamel, Beaumont Hamel
You who nearly broke the back
Of that much-enduring camel
Scottish Jock or English Jack
Rest your cinders on the Grill
Shattered hamlet on the hill.

Ripon Feb. 1917.

CHRISTABEL – A SONG

I

Oh maiden of the sun-fraught hair
And dimpled cheek beyond compare
And eyes of lucent blue
By all the gods I'll freely swear
I ne'er beheld a maid so fair
Till Fortune showed me you.

II

You trip the light fantastic toe
With nymph-like lissomness, and so
My pulse beats like a dynamo
When valsing it with you,
When errant tendrils of your hair
Fanned my hot cheek I do declare
'Twas more than mortal man might dare
To seek those eyes of blue.

III

Come wrack or ruin, fire or flood
'Mid English mist or Picard mud
There is engendered in my blood
A passion sweet as wine
Oh lass you've stol'n the heart o' me
Take, take your welcome mart o' me
Come, come and be a part of me
I'm yours if you are mine.

Christabel, Christabel
How much I love thee, no tongue can tell,
Christabel, Christabel,
Heart o' me, part o' me
I love thee well.

Ripon. Feb. 1917

LIL' GIRL O' MINE

I

I'm feeling most terribly lonely,
Dear lil' girlie o' mine,
As I think of that day when we parted.
From your eyes shone a light divine,
And I think how I clasped your wee fingers
As you whispered a fond farewell;
Then I trudged off back to the barracks
With a heart like a muffled bell.

II

It's two long years since I saw you.
Dear lil' girlie o' mine,
And I dream of wistful yearning
In your quiet grey eyes divine;
When my trail is lone no longer,
And I claim you for my own,
Thro' sunny day or gloamin' grey
We'll go – just we two alone.

Refrain:

I'm feeling most terribly lonely
Weary for want of you
I care not what happens, if only
God grants me those sweet eyes of blue

Oh sweetheart you know how I miss you
My heart will for ever be true
I'm feeling most terribly lonely
Longing for love of you.

Ripon 1917.

THE PRIVATE

I

I'm fed to the teeth with the whole concern
That's what I am,
Treated like blinkin' Board-School kids
Fresh from the pram
Expected to thrive on physical jerks
    'Bully' and jam.

II

Of course I've roughed it the other side
But my bit ain't done
Till the last shot's fired I want to scrap
With the bloody Hun,
It's wonderful what a chap can do
    With a flag and a gun.

III

But when I'm back on the barrack-square
An' steppin' it quick
With a heart like brimstone, feet like fins
Just longin' to kick,
When I see these blokes who've stayed at home
    Gawd! it makes me sick.

THE SERGEANT

It's a rummy job is the sergeant's job
When you come to think it out,
Grousin' at sweatin' soldier-men,
Turnin' them right about,
Or standin' there in the market square
As a darned recruitin' tout.

Of course I was out with the boys at Mons,
An' wounded on the Aisne;
Then swankin' it loud with Kitchener's crowd
On the dreary, dusty Plain;
But a 'whizz-bang' downed me on the Somme
So here I'm back again.

Now they keeps me safe on 'Blighty's' shore,
Where I often longed to be,
An' I still knocks about in a khaki coat,
An' drinks my army tea,
But this tribunal conscript mob
Will soon be the death o' me.

Tho' I'd rather fight 'gainst Prussian might
On the other side of the sea,
This army job is a man's best job,
An' it's here I'm proud to be,
For the thud of butts on the barrack yard
Is meat and drink to me.

Written in hospital at Tidworth. Jan. 1917.

THE SUBALTERN

I

Here I am clad in khaki
Instead of the old red gown
Drilling with Kitchener's army
Fing'ring my top-lip down
But I never thought so last winter
When I bunked in the wee grey town.

II

I think of the smoky Union
With its cluster of men round the fire
Ragging some boon companion
Rousing his friendly ire;
And Sundays in the chapel
Singing to drown the choir.

III

I'd like to be playing rugger
In jersey of faded blue
Or yelling like steam on the tough-line
Itching to be there too.
We've a sterner game before us
And we're going to see it through.

IV

There's not much good in grousing
Work lies here to be done
'Varsity days seem sweetest
Though soldiering's just A.1.
So we'll have a good go at the Germans
Just you wait, won't we make 'em run.

Ripon 1917.
College Echoes 30.10.14.

BACK AGAIN

I

Back to the brunt of the same old Front,
Back to the same old game,
Back to the whine of the Boche five-nine,
(Cursed be Krupp's black name)
Back to the dust and the water-lust
When you know what a thirst can be
With a blistered sole an' a heart like coal
An' eyes too bleared to see.

II

Down in the glade 'neath the fir-trees' shade
Under the great blue tent
Free in their rest lie most of the best
Strong lives gladly lent;
Back to the faith that the turning-lathe
Of the War which made us men
May shape us right for the far-flung fight
To end all strife – but when?

Grande Rullecourt 1917.

LITTLE MARIE

We're going up tomorrow
To the battered battle line;
We're trudgin' up tomorrow,
An' it ain't no use to whine;
For the day is done for resting,
And we drop our joyous jesting
With the bonnie, bright-eyed Marie
In the cot beside the chateau,
Where we loafed the long, long gloamings,
An' we parlez-vooed – 'twas fine.

We're here to do the dirty
On the Germans over there;
They're there to do us dirty,
If the blighters only dare,
When the cool, sweet dawn is breaking
And the guns from sleep are waking,
I shall think of little Marie,
In the orchard near the chateau,
As she sits and samples cherries
With lips like red, red wine.

Dundee Advertiser July 10th 1917.
Sent from the trenches somewhere in France.

BEFORE BATTLE

I

God of the First and Last and Best
Lord of the land and sea,
Aid us now in our warlike quest
Whereso'ever we be.

King, who outkings all earthly kings,
    Guide every heart and hand;
Lead as aright by day or night,
    O'er trench or desert sand.

II

Ours is the hope to win the fight
    And set the whole world free:
Thine is the everlasting might
    That holds the final Key
To that great Door of Fortune's gloom
    Which never stands ajar,
But swings unceasing to and fro
On deeds that men call War.

III

The clangour and the clash of arms
        Make hideous each day;
The earth is marred, and scorched, and torn,
        While hazards throng each way;
Great Father, look upon Thy sons
        Who strive to do Thy will,
And teach us best to merit Rest
Hard by Thy Holy Hill.

Dundee Advertiser – July 23rd 1917.

THE WOODEN CROSS

A broken obelisk, a chiselled heart
Shreds of a dead convention, once
    a part of Life
But now as common dross

A broken tree, a shattered home
Symbols of man-made kultur
    Hate and Strife

God, if it be my lot to lie
Under an alien-tented sky
Let me but share the soldier's shrine
    A Wooden Cross.

THEN – NOW – PERHAPS

Then

Have you ever heard the tinkle
Of the little village-bell,
Have you ever seen the twinkle
Of the young folk down the dell,
When our laughing, joyous revels
Rippled upward towards the sun,
When the earth seemed free of devils
And we'd never heard of 'Hun'?
Summer days of rosy brightness
Dewy dawn to gloaming grey
While the old man of the sickle
Took the toll of work and play.

Now

Have you ever heard the clatter
Of the dixies from afar,
Have you ever seen the spatter
Of a man-created star,
When our anxious sleepless faces
Turning upward to the skies
Wait for Fate to do its duty
In some ugly godless guise?

Summer days of rosy brightness
Crow of cock to candle-light
Wasted, squandered at the altar
Of the creed called ‘Might is Right’.

Is there any need to prattle
Of those days beyond recall?
In the din and stress of battle
Better far forget them all.

Perhaps

But in happy days hereafter
When the curse of War is past,
May the tinkle of our laughter
Glad this sad old land at last.

A SOLDIER'S HOPE

A tot of native cheer, a blackened briar,
And all my life to feel their flavour;
A bed by night, a job by day,
That rest from toil may keep its savour;
    Just now and then.
A fire, a friend, a jolly story.

A decent wife, a cosy home,
A brush that makes a healthy lather;
A few good friends, some cash saved up,
Mayhap a kid who loves his father;
    And at the end
A quiet going out to God.

GAS SHELLS

Whistling, screaming, foul of breath
Winged harbingers of death;
Hurtling through the night
Now on left, now on right.
    Can you hear them, pal
        As they fall
Over yonder by 'the School'?*

God! I breathe the fiendish fume,
And my heart turns sick with spume
    Quick with your mask,
        No time to ask
    Is it a 'dud' pal?
        As they fall
Close and closer still.

Oh! I wish the brutes would stop!
Did you see big Stewart drop?
    What! you fell ill?
    Well, lie quite still
        Never mind them pal
        Tho' they fall,
Close to our feet.

* *A building notorious in recent Flanders Fighting.*

THE CORPORAL'S TALE

I

Now this is a tale of the Lewis Gun
A tale that was told to me
By a corporal tight on a wet, wet night
By the side of the grey North Sea
When the wind blew high in a sullen sky
Across an angry bay
'Mid clink of glass or laugh of a lass
We whiled the hours away.

II

And the corporal told how he dreamt a dream
Of a gun that had all gone wrong
Whose parts were stuck in pools of muck
Whose casing was used as a gong
An' between each creak the parts would speak
To their wrathful Number One
'We don't care a dam if the cartridges jam
In this rotten old Lewis Gun.'

III

Then the feed-arm pawl would pay a call
On the key of the magazine post
An' the locking lugs would hunt for bugs
In the holes where oil lies most
Then the axis pins would kick the shins

Of the actuating stud
An' the piston rod felt rather odd
In a cylinder full of mud.

IV

Then the tangent sight would want to fight
When the circular magazine
And the teeth of the rack would slip right back
Where the sear spring should have been.
The ejector broke in a final stroke
And the butt-stock split with glee,
And the spare-parts bag was smoking a fag
With the regulator key.

V

Now that was the tale of the Lewis Gun
The tale that was told to me
By that Corporal tight that wet, wet night
By the side of the grey North Sea
An' I think in sooth that he told the truth
An' he thought that his tale was true
So the tale that was told by the corporal bold
Is the tale that I've told you.

Viel Hesdin

GOING WEST

I

Yes, I lie here in my 'Blighty' bed,
With some broken bones and an aching head,
A nice wee nurse, and right well fed –
    All o' the best.
But over there where the 'planes fly low,
When the old foe Fritz is loth to go,
There are men I knew, or will never know,
    Goin' west.

II

I've seen men fight, an' I've seen men die,
Hell upon earth and Hell in the sky;
I've looked through the shroud of a doctor's eye –
    'Twas for the best.
Yet here I lie in the clean white bed,
An' my rifle's lost – I've a book instead –
While my poor old pals are facing lead
    Goin' west.

III

In Night of wrath or morn of rue,
A nobler thing men never do –
It might be me – it might be you –
    Goin' west.

Dundee Advertiser 5th September 1917.

MY PICTURE

I have a dug-out,
Corrugated iron overhead,
Wire netting and sand bags for a bed,
An empty bomb box for a table,
For light a candle in a whisky bottle,
And mud, mud, God, what mud! – in it,
Outside it, all round it.

I have a picture in my dug-out,
Not much of a picture,
One of Valentine's coloured post cards,
But it's bonny, oh it's bonny,
When I smoke my pipe and look at it
In fancy free I'm trudging,
Through the woods,
Among the bracken,
Along the granited roads,
In the clean, snell air of a
Scottish morn.

It's just a broken old tree,
Mute symbol of our frailty,
Buffeted by many a storm,
Throned on a hill-top with silent courtiers,
Tall, feathery grasses bending before the wind,
Fleecy cloudlets scurrying along above,
I smell the mud no longer,
My lungs are filled with the wind
Which blows o'er that wild upland.

There is a dark wood in my picture
And there I oft-times go
When the fir-trees smell with sweetness after rain,
Brown bracken fringes the wood
And joyous, I plunge into it;
My clothes glistening with silvery cobwebs
As tho' adorned with gems of Araby.
There's a clearing in my wood,
A dark, damp clearing,
No! I won't think of it,
It's too like Flanders to be wholesome,
I always see the wooden crosses there.

Then I clamber to the hill-top
And stand amid the sweet smelling gorse,
How wonderful, how beautiful!
The grey mists in the valley,
The dusky purple of the heath-clad hills.

But out here,
The landscape is no picture,
It's an ugly travesty of Nature.
Shell holes, stinking shell holes,
Rotting bodies, hungry rats.
And mud, mud – what hellish mud!
All around us like a sea of slime.

ANY SOLDIER – 1918

I

It's not my line to march and fight
But I joined up quick enough,
Might have had four quid a week
Makin' big shells,
Yet somehow I know that I'm doin' right
By the wife and the kids – good stuff
Yes! often I'll swear they've felt the pinch,
It's grit that tells.

II

I never thought that I'd kill a man
But I've done it – with a grin;
I knew damned well I was saving cash
For the land we love.
Oh I wish they'd say what we're fighting for
For Life seems one long Sin
And we blunder on like stupid sheep
With no God above.

GAS

I

When I was a lad
Much pleasure I had
In producing foul odours in labs,
And confining queer gases
In little round glasses
To be later set free – say in cabs.

II

My people were horrid
Their manner was torrid
Which really wasn't a wonder
When I think of the day
In a frolicsome way
I gassed the poor cat – what a blunder!

III

But now I'm a man
And I anxiously scan
The wire and the waste of the trenches,
I gingerly sniff
At each unholy whiff
And I wonder what each filthy stench is.

IV

There's nothing so windy
As the gas-gongs wild shindy
When the east wind is stinging our faces,
The cylinders hissing
Like Satan's host kissing
And we have to stand firm in our places.

V

When war it is over
I'll never smell clover
Without saying 'gas shells' and spitting,
I want no more stink-pot
It's safe with my ink-pot
And a chair that is soft to the sitting.

THE BLIGHTY-THOUGHTS

Dawn – in the trenches

The tuneless thunder of a thousand guns
Has ceased crescendo and its dull refrain
Brings memory of martial squalor; once again
The pale dreams of a Night are swept away
Yet with the chilly struggling Birth of Day
When all the East is flushed with Light
And all the hearths of Heaven are kindled bright
Then shall I come to thee with lips afire
Sweet lady of an ardent heart's desire.

Dusk – behind the lines

Silent are all the mighty dogs of War
Their baying ceased, their sullen voices dumb
And all the world drones with a drowsy hum
Of rest from toil, and respite from the fray.
Then at the close of each tempestuous day
When Man has time to think, perhaps to pray
Then in my dreams I see my lady fair
And toy with tendrils of her lustrous hair.

'At the beginning and end of each day, one's thoughts always flit home for a few moments.'

HIGHLANDERS

THE SEAFORTH RAID

I

The Seaforths made a raid last night
As we were 'standing to'
And in the summer gloamin' light
We saw advancing to the fight
The tartan purple, red and white
And ne'er a face of rue.

II

Mackenzie's men came slowly back
With prisoners one or two
And though the clan lost sore that night
The tartan purple, red and white
Had gloried in a hard-won fight
As Highlanders aye do.

France 1918.

THE SCOTTISH HORSE

A famous regiment of Highland Yeomanry raised by the Duke of Atholl.

I

Men of Atholl, men of Garry
Men from Tummell, men from Tay
Will ye ride out with your chieftain
At the break of morrow's day?
Bonnet gay and bonny trappings
Leather smooth and buckles bright
Will ye ride to meet the foeman?
Will ye worst him in the fight?

II

Men from glen of Killiecrankie
Men from wooded Grandtully braes
We have seen you as you cantered
Through the morning battle-haze.
In the forefront Highland yeoman
Gallop straight though bullets sing
Glad and proud in knightly valour
To bear arms for God and King.

III

We have seen you Men of Atholl
Riding homeward from the fray
Mud-bespattered yet exultant

In the fortunes of the day.
Cavaliers of Scotland's mountains
May thy lustral name ne'er die
While the wild winds shriek o'er Birnam
Where the fir-trees flog the sky.

Argyll & Sutherland Highlanders

THE STIRLIN' LASSIE

I

Your een were dewy-wet, lass
When I left Stirlin' toon
And on your rosy cheek, lass,
A tear-drop wimpled doon,
Oh sad was I to go, lass,
My heart was unco sair
D'ye mind how I looked back, lass
Gaun through the Castle Square?

II

You waved your wee white hand, lass,
And smiled right through your tears,
You made me prood to ken, lass,
Your faith could strangle fears.
The bonnet and the kilt, lass,
That flaunt the 'thin red line'
Are fighting for your sake, lass,
Across the ocean brine.

III

And if I sleep out there, lass,
Just keep a thocht o' me
That wore the braw green kilt, lass,
An' wasna feared tae dee.

POPPIES OF CAMBRAI

I

Why do the poppies bloom so red
Along the Cambrai Road?
Why do the cornflowers sway so fair
Where brave battalions strode?
Is it a tale they tell to me
To ease my load of pain?
Is it a hymn from earth to God
That sweetly quiet refrain?

II

Why do the roses blossom white
Athwart the cobbled way?
Why do they make my heart feel light
Though weary of the fray?
What is it here that fires the soul
That quickens each man's breath?
Is it a song they sing to me
Of deeds that live in death?

III

Red was the blood that dead men shed
Red are the poppies there;
White shone the light of steadfast souls
White bloom the roses fair;
Silent the host by the lone wayside
Noble the tale they tell
Of men who strode that Cambrai Road
To face the powers of Hell.

Ripon.

AN ORDINARY SOLDIER

Out of the mist, and the mire, and the mud
Came a man with a face like chalk,
With eyes red-rimmed in lust for sleep,
And legs that were loth to walk,
And the clothes he wore were stinking wet,
And his tongue could barely talk.

He was fed, he was housed, he was clothed anew,
He was told to clean his gun;
He was washed and lectured and forced to shave,
'Ere each day's work begun;
He was paid; got drunk in a Belgian pub,
The ------ F.P. Number One.

Into the mist, and the mire, and the mud,
Went a man with a face of fire:
Into the jaws of worse than Hell;
Over the bags, through the mangled wire,
With a cheek unshaved and a tunic torn,
And ninepence his daily hire.

A dead man sprawls on the German wire
And a woman weeps by a burnt-out fire.

IF I AM EVER OLD

If I am ever old and grey,
I'll call the children from their play
To cluster round my chair;
And tell them tales about the War,
And see their chubby faces stare.
Then, after they have run away,
I'll chuckle o'er the tales I've told,
    Then light my pipe –
    And maybe pray.

For if the children at their play
Were told the truth, we'd rue the day;
They'd over soon be old;
They'd know the ugliness of War,
By some loquacious veteran told.
So let them laugh and gambol gay
And revel in the tales they've heard.
    While I look on
    As best I may.

Andover Advertiser April 19th 1918.

THERE'S LITTLE ELSE

I

There's little else to do but grouse
When skies are leaden-grey
And all the trees are draggled wet
And fields are clogged with clay;
Out in the rain or dry within a house,
There's little else to do but grouse.

II

There's little else to do but smile
When folk must keep their peckers up,
When battle fronts are changing shape
And Woolwich plays at Death with Krupp;
Although things look dead black awhile,
There's little else to do but smile.

III

There's little else to do but live
If you come scatheless from the fray;
It's up to us to value life.
That we may fight another day.
When men want what we have to give
There's little else to do but live.
But when we've burnt our candles – why,
There's little else to do but die.

THE MONS RIBBON

A red, white and blue ribbon now worn by all soldiers who fought in France before Nov. 23rd 1914.

Just a splash of vivid colour
On a breast of sober drabness.
What a world of meaning there!
Symbol of a nation's trial,
When our sky glowered black as thunder,
And the world was nigh despair.

Red the blood you shed to save us,
White the purpose of your presence,
Blue the watch that keeps our shore.
To the gallant, great Old Army,
Men who wear the '14 Ribbon
Thank you! now and evermore.

Andover Advertiser 22nd March 1918.

THE ROAD TO ARMENTIÈRES

I

The weary road, the dusty road, the road of cobbled stone
Where silent poplars flank the clouds of grime
Where Bill was 'done in' by a crump and I was left alone
And all red Hell was working overtime,
It's left behind with blood and bitter tears
The road that leads through Pont Nieppe to shambled Armentières.

II

The Flemish ditches hold the dead who knew that cobbled way
And tried to stem the torrent of the foe,
They marched to fight for King and Right at one-and-six a day
And what they suffered God alone can know,
They're left behind with blood and bitter tears
Along the road from old Bailleul right up to Armentières.

Down the cobbled road they're straggling through the haze of April rain
Haggard, hungry German legions like bloody sons of Cain.

ITALY

The din of battle on the Lombard plain
Fills all our anxious ears; and not in vain
Italia calls for succour in her stress.
For as of old, ere Rome yet ruled the world
Then Tarquin from his royal seat was hurled
And flew to Tuscan peers for quick redress,
The hosts of Porsena were marshalled all,
From East, West, South and North, Thro' every hall,
Resounded knightly mirth or woman's woe.
Now France and Britain to the rescue fly,
Caparisoned for combat with a ruthless foe.

MAISIE

I

The maids of the West are fair to see
As flowers on a summer day
The Maids of the East are straight and tall
As poplar trees in May.
The maids o' the South are sweet of mouth
As honey from the comb,
But the maid o' the North is my own maid,
Just the lassie who lives near home.

Refrain:
    My maid, shy maid,
Dear to the heart o' me,
    My lass, my lass,
Near to her aye would be
An' oft in the gloamin' I dream that we're roamin'
Out by the links or the sea,
For my wee lassie's a lass frae the North
An' there's no sic another twixt
    Pentlands and Forth.
    I tell you I'm crazy,
    O'er my ain wee Maisie,
    The lass who is fond o' me.

The maid o' my choice is a bonny lass,
An' when she smiles on me
The cockles o' my puir wee heart

Just clink in ecstasy
O'er desert sand, thro' Flanders mud,
Mid perils of the main
I'd go for her thro' fire and blood
Some day she'll be my ain.

Refrain:
    Maisie, Maisie,
Dear to the heart o' me,
    My lass, my lass,
Soon you'll be part o' me,
An' oft in the gloamin' ye'll find us oot roamin'
Oot by the cliffs or the sea.
For my wee lassie's a lassie frae Fife,
An' ye'll ne'er meet a better in a' a man's life.
    I tell ye I'm crazy,
    O'er my ain wee Maisie,
    The lass who's the lass for me.

WHEN I PUT OFF MY KHAKI COAT

I

When I put off my khaki coat and dump my old tin hat
I'll come and claim you darling – don't you worry over that,
A tearful smile will glisten in your tender eyes of blue
When I put off my khaki coat and come right back to you.

II

The sergeant-major says that I am far too pleased to go
I tell him he'd be jealous too, could he but only know
The reason for my hurry and my cheery, happy state,
The little girl that's waiting by the good old garden gate.

Refrain: (after each verse)

You've been wait-wait-waiting by the old stone stile
We'll be mate-mate-mating very soon,
Put the lid on all your sorrow
I'm demobilised to-morrow
And we'll soon be on our honeymoon.
I'll be work-work-working at my civvie job
With a cosy little home for two in view
I'll be fit to burst with pride
When you are by my side
For I'm coming right back to you.

NO OTHER BOY IN THE BIG WIDE WORLD

I

We wandered down the village street
   My little maid and I;
The cobbled stones beneath our feet,
   And sunshine in the sky:
My step was light, my heart was gay,
   For well I knew 'twas true,
No other lad upon that day
   Could love, as I could do.

Refrain:

No other boy in the big wide world
   Can love you more than I,
No other lad has felt so glad
   As I, when I knew what a heart you had;
Love, there is joy in the whole fair earth,
And song in the great blue sky:
No other boy in the big wide world
   Can love you more than I.

II

We wandered back at close of day,
With all the west aglow;
And gaily down the cobbled way,
We heard the children go:

Their laughter echoes in my heart,
   A song in praise of thee;
It was a hallowed eventide,
   For my sweet maid and me.

Refrain:

No other boy in the big wide world
   Can love you more than I,
No other lad has felt so glad
   As I, when I knew what a heart you had.
Love, there is joy in the whole fair earth
And song in the great blue sky.
No other boy in the big wide world
   Can love you more than I.

1919.

MY MEADOWSWEET – A Song

(The 'meadowsweet' or 'queen of the meadows' is a lovely wild flower very little celebrated by writers or verse.)

I

I know a sunny little mead
Where fragrant clover grows
And it is fair as garden rare
Of lavender and rose,
And there I sometimes go alone
Where daisies kiss the feet
While summer breezes gently blow
The scent of meadowsweet.

II

I have a corner in my mead
And there I go alone
Where blooms my gentle meadow-queen
Upon her grassy throne,
The beauties of her little court
My eager senses greet
Most fragrant of wild Nature's flowers
My queenly meadowsweet.

Refrain: (after each verse)

Oh meadowsweet, pale meadowsweet;
What praise will serve thy name to greet?
In all my mead there's none so sweet
As meadowsweet, fair meadowsweet.

THE STARS

I

I mind the nicht I stood wi' her
Beneath the winter stars
An' weel we liked the gleesome glint
O' Venus and O' Mars
For ne'er a thocht was in oor minds
Of pestilence an' wars.

II

Oot here among the Picard glaur
The stars shine jist the same
An' look doon on each wooden cross
That bears a brave lad's name
An link wi' specks o' cauld dear licht
Each sodger's hairt wi' hame.

III

The stars focht in their courses yince
So Israel's prophet's tell
Oh wad oor myriad host of stars
An' auld Man Moon as well
Were man o' might and purpose stem
Tae scourge the hounds o' hell.

IV

But we must dree oor lanesome weird
An' face a gey steep brae
So when the stars glint on the frost
Maist like the licht o' day
I'll aye mind o' that nicht lang syne
By Auld St. Andrews Bay.

ON LEAVING HOSPITAL

And so at last the fateful day has come
When Halls of Healing I no longer tread,
No longer now it is my peaceful lot
To dwell in langour in a sheeted bed
Or garbed in gown of iridescent hue
(Methinks I'd better sack the aid of rhyme
In these my lisping numbers.)
'Twere sublime
To dwell for ever in a sunlit ward
Near by a roaring city, doors unbarred
Tho' cash be scanty, regulations hard.

The laugh of radiant Doddles, Sister Jean,
Of sunny cheek or Flittie's sober mien,
Shades of the days that passed most wondrous well.

And Peggie, what of her? Capricious maid!
The best of friends would scarcely call her staid.
Will she forget the kilt of sombre plaid?
Vale, valete, Whitworth Street, farewell.

Exit L. With Baggage.

Curtain.

'K.P.O.'

(The motto of the British Armies is now 'Keep pushin' on'.)

I

There's a motto that the fighting men keep ever in the van
Of all they try to do by flood and field,
It's a sort of dogged watchword that becomes a British man
An' it's stronger than the strongest arms they wield.
An' the thought of it will brace them in each awful bloody 'show'
When they face the ugly Hell on Earth that only soldiers know.
In the mind of every soldier, Colonel, man or N.C.O.
Dins the grim New Fighter's motto: 'K.P.O.'

II

When our pecker's getting lowish an' we're lumpy at the throat,
When the skies look bilious-yellow overhead,
An' your pal has lost his father on a Glasgow cargo-boat
An' you wonder are the wife and kiddies fed,
Then the dogged battle-motto comes to steal us for the fray
An' we curse our luck quite cheery in the usual sort of way.
For the sign-post on to DUTY, 'brass-hat' man or N.C.O.
Is the grand new British motto: 'K.P.O.'

THE WAACIEST OF WAACS

I

If ever you go walking down the road beside the camp
To watch the little ducks go by or buy a penny stamp
You'll see a lot of girls about in coats of khaki hue
And if you smile to one of them I'm sure she'll talk to you.

II

It's good to see the girlies looking absolutely fit
From top to tootsies cheery 'cos they're out to do their bit,
And if you don't believe it, why just come along and see,
The little Waacs aworking for the sake of you and me.

(After each verse)
Refrain:

When the Waaciest of Waacs
Meets the Khakiest of Khaks
Then there's bound to be a little parley-voo,
He will tell the old, old tale
As they wander down the vale
Till her heart is more a-flutter
Than a rag-time jumble sale.

When the hosiest of hose
Twinkle where the cowslip grows
Then you bet you'll see the soldier-boy pursue
And the Waaciest of Waacs
Knows the Khakiest of Khaks
Is full of beans when e'er he starts to woo.

Late research has discovered that this ditty was put to music and published under the topical title, *My Waac*, by Lieutenant Nat D. Ayer.

CELA NE FAIT RIEN, SI ------

I

Were honey half so sweet
As thy sweet nature
I'd speedily become a bee
And at thy fairy feet
Lay down my treasure
In earnest love for thee.

II

Were roses half so fair
As thy fair visage
A dewdrop speedily I'd be
Those lips so red, so rare
Would know strong homage
Of earnest love for thee.

III

Were Kingdoms half so great
As my ambition
To make thee ever mine
I'd scorn the worldly state
And lay my love's petition
Before my lady's shrine.

THE VISSEE MINE

Vissee trench is a communication trench in the famous 'Labyrinth' near Neuville St. Vaast. The Vissee Mill is one of the most prominent landmarks on the landscape.

I

Ye mind the nicht the mine went up
Near by the Vissee mill
The companies were 'standing to'
In the gloamin' grey an' chill
While the sun glowered down frae yont a cloud
I think I see it still.

II

The earth just heaved, a muckle roar
Rent a' the heavens in twain,
And showers of German shrapnel fell
Like gusts of red-hot rain,
Then in a lull we heard the cries
Of some poor chaps in pain.

III

The Frenchman had a half-made shaft
Where sappers used to go
An' listen tae the Boche at work
That's how we used to know
When to look out an' where to watch
For danger from below.

IV

So when the other mine went up
These sappers 'neath the ground
Were caught like rats in poisoned holes
With danger all around.
We listened at the tunnel top
But couldn't hear a sound.

V

But our brave bombing officer
Went boldly down below
And dragged the smothered Frenchmen out.
Well, most folk surely know
He risked his life to rescue men
With foul gas as their foe.

VI

He won the Military Cross
And France's medal too
Both right well-earned I must say
And so I'm sure will you.
That's how I mind the Vissee Mill
As most our fellows do.

Ripon. Feb. 1917.

SAD EYES

I

Why are your eyes so sad, lass,
When all the world is gay?
Why are your cheeks so pale, lass,
When roses strew our way?
Let me but make thee glad, lass,
With cups of Love's Red wine,
Let me but see thee flush, lass,
As thy lips meet with mine.

II

Come with me through the dusk, lass,
When all the West's aflame,
Walk with a lad you trust, lass,
A lad who is aye the same.
Sable the skies above, lass,
Wayward the path below
But valiant in our Love, lass,
Across Life's night we'll go.

DESIRE

I

Two eyes of bluey-grey
Misty yet full of meaning
As reek o' the battle-plain
To gaze into those depths
'Twere ecstasy,
Shining as stars beneath a summer sea,
But not for me.

II

Two lips of cherry redness,
The luscious fruit of maidenhood;
But trenched and wired
To meet those smiling lips
'Twere bliss,
The proof that someone cared –
A kiss?

SNATCHES OF SONG

I

When the lilac-tree was blooming
And a lovely thing to see
And the linnet whistled snatches
In the old laburnum tree,
You were coy and I was callow
And the world was at our feet,
What a lot of time we wasted!
Are you sorry now, my sweet?

II

When there's honey 'mong the heather
And there's sunshine on the brae
How we tramped the hills together
On that dear dead yesterday.
Did we ever stop to wonder
What our destiny would be?
Oh I'm glad to think we didn't
And I'm sure that you'll agree.

Chateau Hardelot
1.1.19.

THE BOSUN'S WIFE – A SONG

I

When you go out across the bay
And I am left ashore
Oh lonely is the cobbled way
That straggles past my door,
And when the homely fire is lit
I always think of thee
As all alone I muse and knit
When you are out at sea.

Refrain:
When you are sailing far away
Across the ocean free
I wander down the cobbled way
And stand beside the sea,
And though the billows of the deep
May keep us far apart
In waking dreams or in my sleep
Your face is near my heart.

II

When you sail back across the bay
And I am there to greet
There's sunshine down the cobbled way
Beneath my happy feet.
The little home we call our own

Is filled with joy for me
For I am never quite alone
When you are home from sea.

Refrain:
When you are sailing far away
Across the ocean free
I wander down the cobbled way
And gaze across the sea,
But when my love is by my side
Each twilight down we go
To where beside the little pier
The waves are coming low.

Ripon.

THE LILAC TREE

I

There are roses in my garden
There's a thrush in the lilac tree
There are stars of love in the skies above
But none so fair as thee.
There's a hush in the scented twilight
And music on the breeze
And of fairies in a Dreamland
  Afloat on dreaming seas.

II

Were you but in my garden
We twain 'neath the lilac tree
When lips divine are close to mine
  I'll prove my love for thee.
I'd joy in your shy caresses
And the hot sweet scent of your hair
Like the fragrant breath of the rain-kissed heath
On the summer moorland air.

III

So when you leave my garden
And I am left alone
Beneath the stars I'll thank my God
  That you are still my own.

Catterick. 10.4.18.

HURSTBOURNE PARK

The fragrance of the fresh-cut grass
The glory of the summer skies,
Make all the world a sheer delight.
The frolic of each dusky lamb,*
In joyous gambol by its dam,
Is but a symbol of our right,
To laugh and play and sing glad songs
When trees are green and skies are bright.

The copper-beech of burnished glow
Looks down to where sweet tulips grow,
And sunbeams kiss the silvered birchen tree;
Quiet lilacs whisper soft and low
To modest daisies far below,
All fresh and white and fair to see,
While clear across the wooded park
The linnet's love-song comes to me.

May 9th, 1918

* *Black St. Kilda sheep are kept in Hurstbourne Park.*

ON THE BRAID HILLS

The hills are flecked wi' yellow gorse
    O' fragrance honey-sweet,
That like a draught of Druid's mead
    My troubled senses greet.
Gone are the thoughts of war and hate,
    Of triumph or defeat.

Were you but here among the hills,
    And none near to see,
The glory of the sun-kissed gorse
    Would throne my queen for me,
And every linnet down the haugh
    Would warble songs of thee.

The braes will soon be lush wi' dew,
    The skies are settlin' grey;
And all the summer gloamin' hush
    Tells of a tired old day.
'Twere sacrilege to prattle now
    Upon the homeward way.

The Black Watch.

I WISH

– some nonsensical rhymes.

I

I wish I were a hermit
And living in a cave
Amid the rocks and boulders
Hard by the sad sea wave.
I'd wear my very oldest clothes
And hardly ever shave.

II

I wish I were a botanist
And naming pretty flowers
In some Botanic Gardens
For hours and hours and hours,
And if I found a blossom
Bedecked in royal blue
I'd plant it in my window-box
And call it 'Saucy Sue'.

MARIE

There's a dirty little cottage
Down beside the old canal
And if you're going down that way
Just stop and pay a call
For then you'll meet our Marie
  Ever-smiling little Marie,
Who is liked by one and all.

The cottage may look dirty
When you face its battered door
But it's like a breath of Blighty
When you smell the clean-scrubbed floor,
For she works hard, little Marie,
  Conscientious little Marie
And what does man like more?

Little Marie isn't lovely
Like a lady of the stage
But her grey eyes twinkle sweetly
And her 'egg-flip' is quite the rage,
So let's drink the health of Marie
  Honest, happy little Marie
May she reach a ripe old age.

Beaumarais.

TO MARY – another man's girl

Were honey half so sweet
As thy sweet nature
I'd speedily become a bee
And lay my treasures at thy feet
In earnest hope that I were then
A worthier mate for thee.

TO NORA – an Irish girl.

If I but knew how much you cared
And if your roguish smile
Was but the mirror of a loving heart
And not a piece of guile,
I'd steal you from the other man
And hold you very near
Then if you laughed and ran away
I'd say 'Good-bye my dear'.

But if you said 'I love you, boy'
I'd spend my days in wild and heavenly joy.

Beaumarais.

These two scraps were written to amuse two love-lorn swain.

AIN'T IT ALL A BLEEDIN' SHAME?

I

There's a Mother down in London
An' a widow in Dundee,
There's a flat right in the city
An' a cottage by the sea,
Where the memory of a loved one
Is the shadow of a name
- Gave his life for Britain's glory –
Ain't it all a bleedin' shame?

II

There's a son lies west of Wipers
There's a husband by Bapaume,
More than half a million Britons
Lying 'neath the Flanders loam,
Young lives thrown about like water
While we wonder who's to blame.
Yes! we struggled an' we suffered
Ain't it all a bleedin' shame?

III

Now they talks of an Election
Just to change the country's coat
An' those cursed jingo papers
They will tell us how to vote,

It's high time the nation's fighters
Had an interest in the game
We can sack the wind-bag blighters
Which is not a bleedin' shame.

IV

An' if the country fails us
Well, it isn't worth its name
An' they'll hear our throaty mutter
Ain't it all a bleedin' shame?

Somewhere in France.
28.8.18.

MY SONG SHALL BE OF THEE

I

My song shall be of thee,
        My lady fair,
My soul hath need of thee
        Beyond compare,
And all the long night through
I sigh for thee, cry for thee, die for thee,
To make thee all mine own
My song shall be of thee
        Of thee alone.

II

My dreams are all of thee,
        My lady fair,
My hopes are all for thee
        If you but care.
And with the streak of dawn
I sing to you, cling to you, bring to you
        My heart laid bare
My song shall be of thee
        My lady fair.

Chateau Hardelot.
1.1.19.

COMIC VERSE COMPETITION

ON LEAVING HARDELOT

After the Armistice the First Army School was transformed into an educational institution to equip officers for return to the Universities.

At last I ween the fateful day has come
When Halls of Learning I no longer tread,
No longer shall I hear the morning drum
Or leap reluctant from a flea-bag bed;
No longer hear Bill Bailey bellow 'shun!'
Or see fair Fanny make his great salute
Or curse the remnant of that breakfast egg
Upon the lips of some poor 'second loot'.
No more shall I admire the old brown jug
Immortalised by Harley, loved by all,
No more shall I endure the work-room 'fug'
Or freeze in silence in the lecture-hall.

O shades of many a dear dead yesterday!
May you remain hard by me when I go
To shed my garb of khaki and of war
Far from the ancient Chateau Hardelot.

THE VALE OF DREAMS

I

There's a valley not far from here
It's the vale of dreaming
And there I sleep when the moon is high
And the stars are gleaming.
Fairies are singing for you and me
Joybells are ringing across the lea,
Happy the hours I spend with thee
In the wonderful valley of dreams.

II

There's a castle not far away
In the vale of dreaming
And there my love has a garden fair
With gay flow'rs teeming.
When I am weary I wander there
Off'ring my lady a heart laid bare,
Praising her eyes, her lips, her hair,
In the wonderful valley of dreams.

Refrain: (after end verse)
I'm dreaming, I'm dreaming, I'm dreaming of you
I care not whether the skies are grey
Your sweet face shining will light my way.
I'm scheming, I'm scheming
To make you all my own

Come down the beautiful valley of dreams –
With me alone.

Aberdeen
30.4.19.

A REVERIE

Were we but up among the hills, we twain alone,
No memory of a broken-fingered town
In shambled Flanders would engloom my mind
With thoughts of War and Hate and Pestilence,
And from the hills, sweet solace would I find,
Scent o' the heather, wimplin' o' the burn
And all the music of the moorland glen,
Would tell me of the happy days to come.
Does Fortune's barque but sail within my ken.
The sun soft-shining on your dusky hair,
Near to my side 'neath the skies of dreamy blue,
The glamour of your dear sweet presence
Make my pulse beat in unison with you.
With wedded hands and mated thought we wander,
Down the steep brae that flanks the silvery Dee,
Your brown eyes sparkle, smile or ponder,
– Oh but it's good to ramble thus with thee!

Were we but up among the hills, we twain alone.

Aberdeen. 1.5.19.

THE BRAES O' BIELDSIDE

I

Oh bonnie are the Bieldside braes
Athwart the silvery Dee,
'Twas there I met my Marian
And Marian met me,
And as we passed the time of day
I liked the shy but winsome way
She turned to me as though to say
'There's no one near to see'.

II

Oh bonnie was the linnet's lay
Frae oot the birchen tree
As we gaed oot that morn in May
Across the daisied lea,
And as I wasna' quite sae blate
When sitting by the five-bar gate
We kissed in quite ecstatic state,
My 'Marian' an' me.

Cults. 2.5.19.

Marian became the author's wife and in due time, my mother.
I.L.T.

A large Sanatorium stands high among the fir woods above Banchory and one wood in particular is always silent as the grave.

THE WOOD OF TEARS

On visiting a sick friend at Banchory Sanatorium

I

A black wood glowers abune the brae
Dark as a Nubian nicht
And there nae children ever play
Or lovers take delicht,
Nae birdies whustle blithe an' gay
Nae squirrels loup wi' glee
An' hardly does the licht o' day
Glint on each sombre tree.

II

Its silence has a sough o' Death,
An' whiles I wander there
Tae tak' a sort o' solemn breath,
For what can man dae mair
When standin' in a kirk o' gloom
Wi' stately pillars roond,
'Mid silence greater than the tomb
An' ne'er a heartsome soond.

III

Oh! when I tread the causie'd way
That leads to kingdom come
I'll gang richt through that sombre wood
An' hear the muffled drum
That summons me frae trauchle sair
An' loves, an' hates, an' fears,
To somewhere in the Land o' Licht
Far frae the wood o' tears.

Banchory Woods.
10.5.19.

THE KIRK THAT GLOWERS OWRE A'

I

There stands a wee bit granite kirk
Upon a lonely hill
And often in the gloamin' mirk
When a' the world is still
The fairies seem to sob and sigh
Abune her sacred green
And I am waesome as a ghaist
On cauld, dreich winter's e'en.

II

A stony path winds up the brae
An' ilka Sabbath morn
The auld folk clim' wi' rev'rent care
That causeway holy-worn.
A lump aye rises in my throat
When I come down that way
An' think o' days I spent wi' her
That dear dead yesterday.

III

For at the yett that breaks the wa'
She said I was her ain
An' syne we plighted oor sweet troth
For Love had come to reign.

But noo she sleeps the long last sleep
Ayont the kirkyaird wa'
The wee kirk glowers abune her heid
An' fills my soul with awe.

IV

There stands a wee bit glowrin' kirk
    Upon a lonely hill
And always in the gloamin' mirk
    My heart abides there still.

Cults.
May 1919.

MHAIRI DHU

I

Oh Mhairi Dhu the coots are calling
Across the loch and up the whinny brae,
Oh Mhairi Dhu, it's to you they're calling
To meet your lover in the gloamin' grey.

II

My boatie cleaves the soft dark waters
An oars make silver in the sombre wave
An' I am speeding lass to greet you
As warrior would from out his mountain cave.
The firs have cast their long black shadows
The hills are crested wi' the mist o' sleep
An' I am hast'ning on to meet my darling
My gloamin' tryst wi' her tae keep.

III

I see you standing on the moonlit shingle
I hear you singing to the loch we love
In every vein I feel the hot blood tingle
And none knows except the moon above.
A moment's space and I shall rush to greet you
With tender word and passionate caress
And we will wander far along the lochside
– Mayhap the God above will stoop and bless.

IV

Oh Mhairi Dhu, the coots are calling
Across the loch and up the whinny brae
Oh Mhairi Dhu, it's us they're calling
To hail our trysting in the gloamin' grey.

V

My boatie's waiting in the cold dark shadows
And yonder beams the light upon the brae
The oars will soon be swinging through the water
To bear your lad upon his homeward way.
We'll meet again upon this sacred shingle
While fairies flutter softly through the glade
And we shall kiss and you'll be mine for ever
And we'll be happy in our promise made.

VI

Oh Mhairi Dhu, the coots are calling
Across the loch and up the whinny brae,
Oh lassie dear it's me they're calling
To leave my Mhairi in the gloamin' grey.

St. Andrews 1919.

THE HUE O' ROSES

I

The rosy-tinted wine of love
Was surely sent from Heav'n above
    To glad the heart of man and maid
For had we not that wine-like sip
Which trembles on each darling's lip
    Oh! sore athirst we'd be and staid.

II

The rosy-coloured flush of Love
Was surely sent from skies above
    That man might see and know
Without the aid of speech or pen
The radiance of his goddess when
    She feels her passion glow.

III

The rosy-fragrant dreams of Love
Were surely sent by Moon above
    To bring the quiet sleep
Of faith and hope and heart care-free
That day or night and land or sea
    Her promise she will keep.

IV

The rose-embowered life of Love
Is as a gift of God above
    And sacred as the soul
Unsullied may it ever be
And boundless as the mighty sea
    Unto the final Toll.

V

The hue o' roses men may read
Is background for the poet's creed
    Of Love and Fire and Death,
If any know a better flower
To soothe in each and every hour
    Pray let his thought have breath.

VI

The rosy spectacle of Youth
May cover up the naked truth
    Or hide the yellow streak
But if it be a blessed thing
To hear men laugh or maidens sing
    These words I fain would speak.

VII

The clasp of hand, the sunny smile
Are really never worth our while
Than in the rosy light of Love.

AT A DANCE

I

She wore a ribbon in her hair
To match her eyes of blue,
Methinks it were a clever thing
For any maid to do
For Harmony in ball-room dress
Is worth a lot you must confess.

II

He had a sparkle in his eyes
To match his manner gay,
His brain was full of cheery lies
In much the usual way,
For Piquancy in ball-room chat
Ne'er killed the old proverbial cat.

III

They weren't very much apart
So far as I could see
And somehow played the game of Heart
With quite a lot of glee
For 'joie de vivre' to be worth while
Takes little count of Time or Style.

St. Andrews 1919.

KATRINE

I

Oh! rowan-hued are Katrine's lips
And raven-black her hair,
And grey her eyes as winter skies
There's not a maid so fair.
But oh the face belies the heart
And I am left alone,
To see the other by her side
While God hears not my moan.

II

Oh! sweet as mead is Katrine's smile
And loving is her air,
And sweet to touch is her soft cheek
As rose beyond compare;
But oh her heart is hard as stone
And fickle as the wind
She dallies with the other lad
While I am left behind.

III

Oh curses on your bonny face
That lives an endless lie!
Yet never I'll lose hope of you
Until the day I die.

St. Andrews 1919.

THE HEDONIST

As when a sleek complacent cow
Erstwhile replete with clover-tops
Reclines amid the meadow-grass
And chews the ruminative cud
In blank contentment, nigh to sleep,
Though myriad images whirl and pass;

So I within a deep arm-chair
By cheerful hearth renounce all care
In flannel bags and shabby slippers;
Puff pensively the battered briar
And sniff from my landlady's fire
The homely smell of sizzling kippers.

Christmas 1919.

NOSTALGIA

'I'm feeling homesick, sir,' she said
And sadly hung her queenly head,
The while we danced with sleepy step
The last long waltz together.
'Oh shame! Cheer up!' to her quoth I,
'The sun will soon shine in your sky
To-morrow homewards you will fly
Despite the horrid weather.'

II

'You've never known desire's sweet pang
To smell the dear old Bay's salt tang
When College Chapel – or Prof. Fang
Fleet by in misty dreaming.
It is the pang St. Andrews men
Can feel e'en in the farthest ken
And Andrew calls his gownsmen, when
We see his Cross a-gleaming.

III

His crooked cross, his bleeding hand
Can summon us from distant land
To swell again the loyal band
And shout abroad his glory;
Our gowns the emblem of his blood –
But here I stopped – she understood

And said as only Woman would,
'Thanks awfully for your story'.

IV

And when the merry host was fled
I wandered weary home to bed
Her words still ringing in my head
'I'm feeling homesick, sir,' she said.

St. Andrews 1919.

ON THE PIER

The cliffs are crested with the mist of sleep
And silent sail the ships that throng my dreams,
On such a night as this methinks it seems
Our poet Murray gazes o'er the deep
And by our side with ever-willing aid
Tells us the story of his hopes and fears,
The moments of sheer joy, the wasted years
The morn of bitter rue, the winsome maid.
And we are torn by fevered restless thought
That cries to be writ down in words of gold
As lisping numbers struggle to be wrought
That man may know a rare old story told.
– Awed at our phantasy we climb the brae
And silent stride upon the homeward way.

St. Andrews 19.1.20.

IN MEMORIAM

John H. Wilson D. Sc.

Our fathers told us how you shared
With them the hallowed scarlet gown
And glimpsed the world of Men and Books
Within the College of this town.
Wrote verses of a quiet strain
And lived a sober decent life,
A little work, a little play,
And rather more of peace than strife.

We know you as an honest man
Whose daily task seemed always bright,
Who loved his work nor let it flag
From crow of cock to candle-light.
We miss you as a splendid friend
Who spent his days near Andrew's shrine;
And leaves his treasure for our good,
A soul sincere, a heart benign.

So now your sail has braved its last broad sea
We stand upon the Pier and mourn for thee.

St. Andrews 1920.

TO THE 'VARSITY COAT OF ARMS

The blazoned blue and white
Of sainted Andrew's holy Cross;
And eager for the fight
The rampant Lion of Scotland;
High up above where all may see
An open Book, a bishop's gold seal;

These be the symbols of the grey old Halls
Who shield us 'neath the shadow of their towers
And make us men.
The Cross is reared aloft to guide our steps,
The Book is opened to enhance our minds,
The Lion roars its challenge in our ears
To quit a life of tim'rous doubts and fears,
To hold our heads on high and proudly walk
The paths wherein our forebears oft have strode.

St. Andrews 1920.